BRANCH LINES TO SEATON AND SIDMOUTH

Vic Mitchell and Keith Smith

First published September 1991

ISBN 0 906520 95 9

Design and laser typesetting -
            Deborah Goodridge

Published by Middleton Press
            Easebourne Lane
            Midhurst
            West Sussex
            Tel: (0730) 813169

Printed & bound by Biddles Ltd,
            Guildford and Kings Lynn

CONTENTS

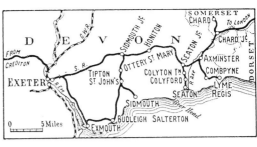

(Railway Magazine)

ACKNOWLEDGEMENTS

In addition to the many photographers credited in the captions, we have received help from Dr.E.Course. D.Cullum, A.Gardner, N.Langridge, N.J.Pomfret, G.Robbins, D.Salter, E.Staff, N.Stanyon, R.White and E.Youldon. We are extremely grateful for this assistance and for the continuing support of our wives.

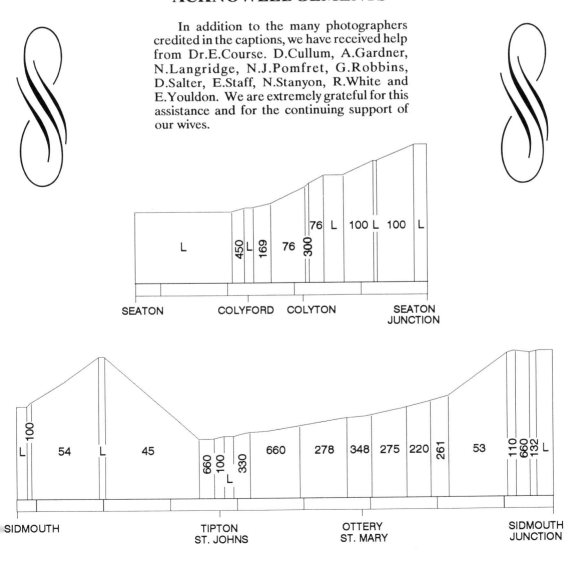

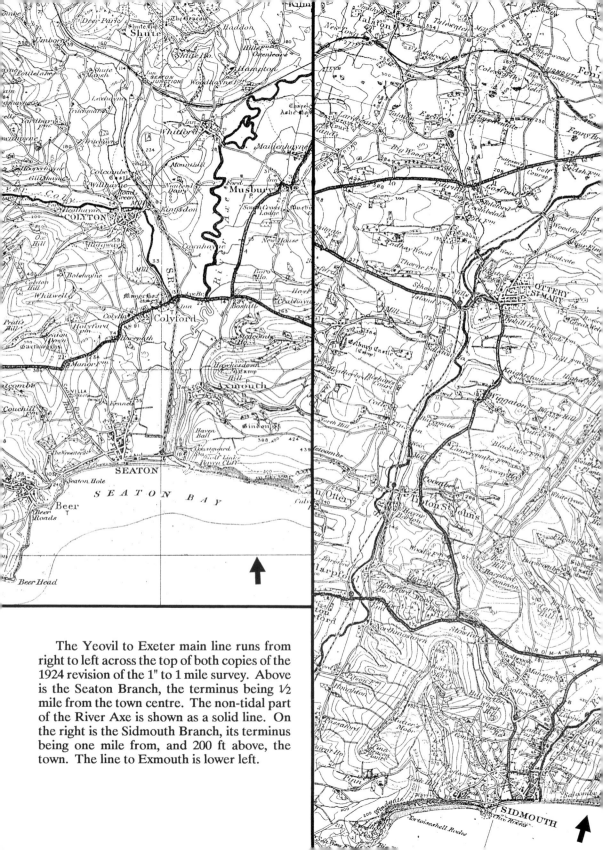

The Yeovil to Exeter main line runs from right to left across the top of both copies of the 1924 revision of the 1" to 1 mile survey. Above is the Seaton Branch, the terminus being ½ mile from the town centre. The non-tidal part of the River Axe is shown as a solid line. On the right is the Sidmouth Branch, its terminus being one mile from, and 200 ft above, the town. The line to Exmouth is lower left.

GEOGRAPHICAL SETTING

Seaton Branch

The entire route was laid on the Alluvium of three valleys. Seaton Junction was situated in the valley of the Umborne Brook, (through which the main line climbs to Honiton Tunnel), which joins the valley of the River Coly at Colyton. The line ran parallel to this river, which flows into the River Axe at Colyford. The broad valley of the Axe was then followed to the coast at Seaton.

Sidmouth Branch

Like the Seaton line, this route was mainly in a valley surrounded by red Keuper Marl. This material carried the final two miles of the branch to its terminus at Sidmouth. Apart from its first mile and last two miles, the route was in the deep valley of the River Otter.

All maps are to the scale of 25" to 1 mile, unless otherwise stated.

HISTORICAL BACKGROUND

The London and South Western Railway's main line opened between Yeovil Junction and Exeter for passenger trains on 18th July 1860. Goods service commenced on 1st September of that year. Single track initially, the doubling was completed within ten years.

Other events to affect both branches were the formation of the Southern Railway in 1923 and British Railways in 1948, the area coming within the Southern Region initially. The lines were transferred to the Western Region on 1st January 1963.

Seaton Branch

The Seaton & Beer Railway Company received its Act on 13th July 1863, the line coming into use on 16th March 1868. The LSWR provided the trains from the outset and acquired the railway on 3rd January 1888.

Diesel services were introduced on 4th November 1963 but the branch closed completely on 7th March 1966. On 28th August 1970, a 2ft 9ins gauge electric tramway was opened on part of the former trackbed near Seaton. The track was extended north to Colyford on 9th April 1971 and to Colyton on 8th March 1980.

Sidmouth Branch

The Act for the Sidmouth Railway & Harbour Company was passed on 7th August 1862 but no further progress was made after 1869, when the company collapsed. A fresh Act on 29th June 1871 resulted in the formation of the Sidmouth Railway and an agreement with the LSWR to work the line. Opened on 6th July 1874, the line maintained its independence until 1922, although always operated by its main line neighbour.

A new line from Tipton was opened to Budleigh Salterton on 15th May 1897, this being extended to Exmouth on 1st June 1903.

The lines were dieselised in November 1963 but the resulting economies failed to avert closure, which took place on 6th March 1967 for passengers and 8th May following for coal traffic.

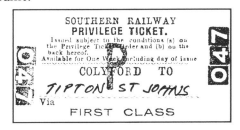

LUNCHEON TICKET
2/6
In conjunction with Excursion
from Seaton (S. Rly.)
This ticket to be surrendered
to the Dining Car Attendant before
Luncheon is served.

PASSENGER SERVICES

Seaton Branch

Initially there were five return journeys, weekdays only, increasing to six in 1868 and eight in the summer of 1869. In 1874 there were seven, 1887 nine and by 1906 there were ten trains each way, this frequency being maintained in 1914. Wartime economies reduced the service to six trains in 1917 but by 1924 it was back to nine, with an extra up journey on Fridays. The 1928 timetable showed 12 weekday trains, with 8 on Sundays. In 1934 there were 12 daily. Reduction in World War II was only slight - 10 weekday and 6 Sunday trains being provided. By 1947 this had been restored to 13 and 6, with two extra trains on Saturdays. A similar service operated in the 1950s, with one or two extra trains in some years. For about 30 years a feature of the timetable had been one through train to and from Axminster on weekdays. The winter Sunday service was withdrawn in September 1950.

The optimum frequency was in 1959 with 15 weekday journeys, 10 on Sundays and three extra on Saturdays. Reductions followed, only to be restored with the advent of diesel units. In the summer of 1965 there were 13 trains on weekdays with 8 on Sundays and three additional trips on Saturdays, but through coaches to London had ceased in 1963.

Sidmouth Branch

The first timetable showed seven weekday trains, a Sunday service not being introduced until the late 1920s. Within six months of opening, the service was reduced to six return trips but by 1890 there were eight, this gradually increasing to eleven by 1914. Wartime savings cut this to seven in 1917, but by 1924 this frequency had been doubled.

The 1928 holidaymaker was offered 16 trains on weekdays and 10 on Sundays, a similar pattern operating until WWII. During 1944, the number was limited to 12 and 6 respectively but post-war timetables were nearly to the same level as pre-war.

The last summer of steam operation (1963) produced 16 weekday trains, with 13 on Sundays and 3 extra on Saturdays. The diesel timetable gave 11 weekday journeys (plus one trip to and from Exmouth), with eight additional trains on Saturdays. There were 10 on Sundays. By 1965, Sidmouth had 14 weekday arrivals, two running from Exeter Central and one from Exmouth. Through trains to London ran on Saturdays only in the summers of 1964 and 1965.

The final summer timetable (1966) had only seven weekday down trains (11 on Saturdays), with six on Sundays.

The above notes omit trains between Sidmouth Junction and Exmouth, which considerably enhanced the service at Tipton St. Johns and Ottery St. Mary.

The figures given for both branches are for down trains, the up service being similar but not identical, as some balancing movements were for freight only.

July 1914

July 1906

Seaton Branch
SEATON JUNCTION

A station was provided here when the main line opened in 1860 but was named "Colyton for Seaton" until the branch came into use in 1868, when it was described as "Colyton Junction". Doubling of the main line took place at about that time. This 1904 map has the line to Honiton on the left, to Axminister on the right and Seaton at the bottom. Note that until 1927, trains from the branch had to reverse into a bay platform. The crane marked was of 5-ton capacity.

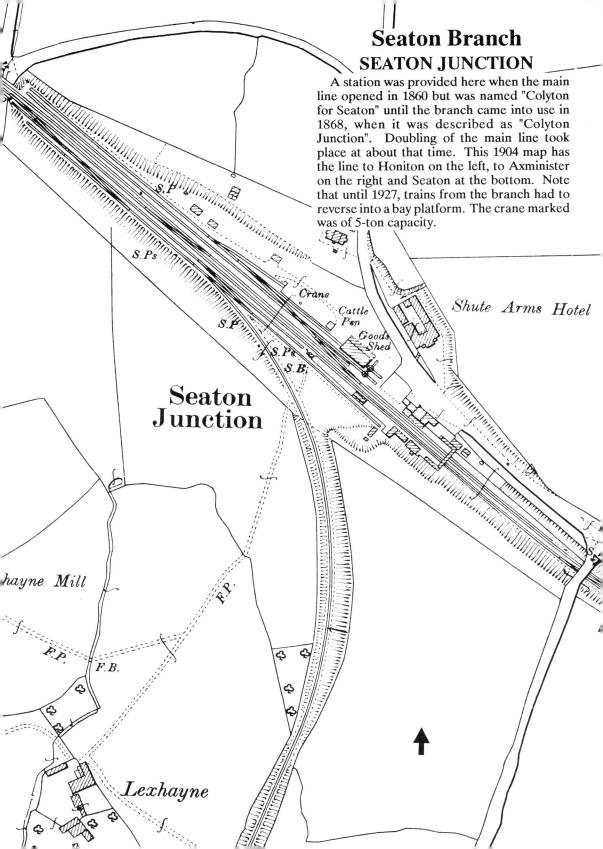

Shute Arms Hotel

Crane

Cattle Pen

Goods Shed

S.P.

S.Ps

S.P.

S.P.

S.P.

S.B.

Seaton Junction

hayne Mill

F.P.

F.P.

F.B.

Lexhayne

1. The "B" above the number indicated that the engine was of Brighton origin. Another member of the LBSCR class D1 (no.B234) was the first to be tried on the branch (on 29th January), its air braking and air operated push-pull equipment proving successful. Regular working by air control commenced on 19th June 1930. In the background is the then new footbridge. (Lens of Sutton)

2. The station was extensively rebuilt in 1927-28, this curved platform on the branch coming into use on 13th February 1927. Class 0415 no. 30584 and class M7 no. 30055 are seen on 18th June 1949, with the 9.0am Seaton to Waterloo train. (S.C.Nash)

3. The rebuilding included provision of two through lines, which gave the only opportunity for trains to overtake (without reversal) between Yeovil and Exeter. No. 34026 (named *Yes Tor* in 1955) and no. 35023 *Holland - Afrika Line* arrive with the heavy 12.20pm Ilfracombe to Waterloo service on 17th June 1949. On the left, class N15 no. 30455 is at the head of the 12.46pm Salisbury to Exeter Central and is detaching the Waterloo-Seaton through coaches. (S.C.Nash)

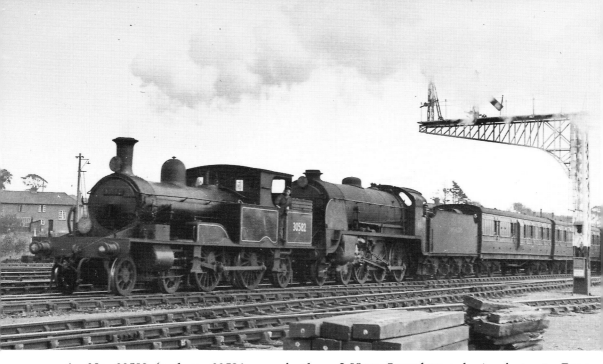

4. No. 30582 (and no. 30584, seen in the picture before last) spent most of its time on the branch line to Lyme Regis (see *Branch Line to Lyme Regis*). It is seen with class S15 no. 844, on the same day, at the head of the 2.08pm Saturdays only Axminster to Barnstaple Junction stopping train, working its way back to its depot at Exmouth Junction. The Seaton branch is in the foreground. (S.C.Nash)

SEATON JUNCTION and SEATON

Miles	Down		am	am	am	am	pm	pm	pm	pm	pm	pm	K	pm	pm	pm	pm	pm		S	am	am	am	am
			Mondays to Fridays																	Saturdays				
—	**Seaton Junction**	dep	**8 10**	**8 49**	**9 44**	**1030**	**12 1**	**1236**	**1 5**	**2 5**	**2 55**	**3 25**	**4 47**	**5 31**	**6 38**	**7 5**	**8 3**	**8 44**	..	**7 30**	**8 10**	**8 42**	**9 42**	**1035**
1½	Colyton		8 14	8 53	9 48	1034	12 5	1240	1 9	2 9	2 59	3 29	4 51	5 35	6 42	7 9	8 7	8 48	....	7 34	8 14	8 46	9 46	1039
2½	Colyford		8 17	8 56	9 51	1037	12 8	1243	1 12	2 12	3 2	3 32	4 54	5 38	6 45	7 12	8 10	8 51	..	7 37	8 17	8 49	9 49	1042
4¼	**Seaton**	arr	**8 20**	**8 59**	**9 54**	**1040**	**1211**	**1246**	**1 15**	**2 15**	**3 5**	**3 35**	**4 57**	**5 41**	**6 48**	**7 15**	**8 13**	**8 54**	....	**7 40**	**8 20**	**8 52**	**9 52**	**1045**

Down		M		N	P	pm	pm	pm	pm	pm	pm	pm	pm	pm		am	am	pm	pm	pm	pm	pm	pm	pm	pm	pm
		Saturdays—*continued*														Sundays										
Seaton Junction	dep	**1127**	..	**1250**	**153**	**2 5**	**320**	**412**	**448**	**534**	**6 38**	**7 5**	**8 3**	**8 44**	..	**1036**	**1110**	**1215**	**2 30**	**3 37**	**4 20**	**625**	**723**	**8 5**	**927**	**1022**
Colyton		1131	....	1254	...	2 10	324	416	452	538	6 42	7 9	8 7	8 48	....	1040	1114	1219	2 34	3 41	4 24	629	727	8 9	931	1026
Colyford		1134	..	1257	.	2 13	327	419	455	541	6 45	7 12	8 10	8 51	..	1043	1117	1222	2 37	3 44	4 27	632	730	812	934	1029
Seaton	arr	**1139**	....	**1 0**	**2 5**	**2 16**	**330**	**422**	**458**	**544**	**6 48**	**7 15**	**8 13**	**8 54**	....	**1046**	**1120**	**1225**	**2 40**	**3 47**	**4 30**	**635**	**733**	**815**	**937**	**1032**

Miles	Up		am	am	L	am		pm	pm	pm	pm	pm	pm	pm	pm	pm		am	am	am	am		Q	am
			Mondays to Fridays															Saturdays						
—	**Seaton**	dep	**7 50**	**8 26**	**10 0**	**1140**	..	**1216**	**1250**	**1 37**	**2 30**	**3 46**	**5 9**	**6 10**	**741**	**8 18**	..	**7 50**	**8 26**	**9 15**	**9 55**	..	**1020**	**11 7**
1¾	Colyford		7 55	8 31	10 5	1145	....	1221	....	1 42	2 35	3 51	5 14	6 15	746	8 23	....	7 55	8 31	....	10 0	....	....	1112
2¾	Colyton		7 59	8 35	10 9	1149	..	1225	..	1 46	2 39	3 58	5 18	6 19	750	8 27	..	7 59	8 35	9 22	10 4	..	..	1116
4¼	**Seaton Junction**	arr	**8 3**	**8 39**	**1013**	**1153**	....	**1229**	**1 0**	**1 50**	**2 43**	**4 4**	**5 22**	**6 23**	**754**	**8 31**	....	**8 3**	**8 39**	**9 26**	**10 8**	....	**1031**	**1120**

Up		pm	pm	R	pm	pm	pm	pm	pm		pm	pm		am	am	am	pm	pm	pm	pm	pm	pm	pm	pm
		Saturdays—*continued*												Sundays										
Seaton	dep	**12 5**	**1 26**	**2 35**	**2 48**	**3 47**	**4 27**	**5 9**	**6 10**	..	**7 41**	**8 18**	..	**1015**	**1051**	**1132**	**2 8**	**3 0**	**3 52**	**6 0**	**6 48**	**7 40**	**9 5**	**9 53**
Colyford		1210	1 31	....	2 53	3 52	4 32	5 14	6 15	....	7 46	8 23	....	1020	1056	1137	2 13	3 5	3 57	6 5	6 53	7 45	9 10	9 58
Colyton		1214	1 35	..	2 57	3 56	4 36	5 18	6 19	..	7 50	8 27	..	1024	11 0	1141	2 17	3 9	4 1	6 9	6 57	7 49	9 14	10 2
Seaton Junction	arr	**1218**	**1 39**	**2 46**	**3 1**	**4 0**	**4 40**	**5 22**	**6 23**	....	**7 54**	**8 31**	....	**1028**	**11 4**	**1145**	**2 21**	**3 13**	**4 5**	**613**	**7 1**	**7 53**	**9 18**	**10 6**

K Through Carriages from Waterloo, dep 1 0 pm **L** Through Carriages to Waterloo, arr 1 50 pm, Mondays and Fridays from 16th July, 2 15 pm on other dates **M** Through Carriages from Waterloo, dep 8 3 am, until 25th August **N** Through Carriages from Waterloo, dep 9 0 am **P** Through Carriages from Waterloo, dep 10 45 am **Q** Through Carriages to Waterloo, arr 1 57 pm **R** Through Carriages to Waterloo, arr 6 13 pm **S** 14th July to 11th August.

June 1962

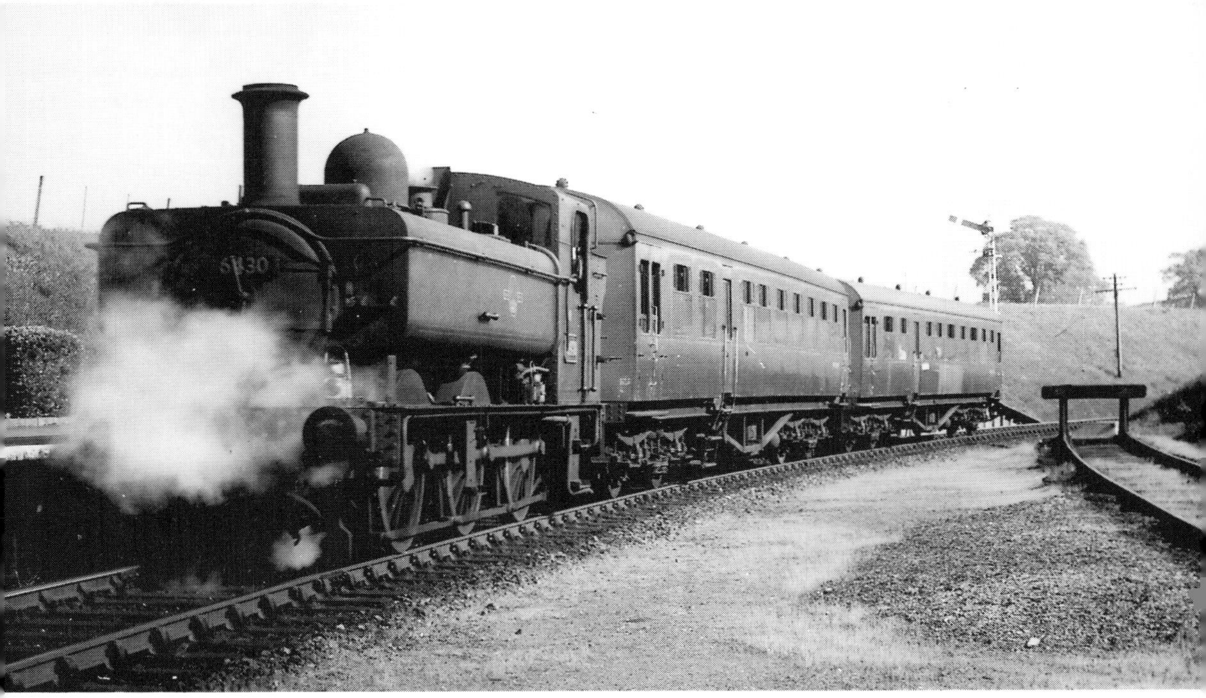

←

5. Class M7 0-4-4T no.30048 was one of a number of members of this class to work the branch and is seen with the 6.10pm from Seaton on 12th August 1960. The footbridge was one of two at the station, this one carrying a public footpath to Lexhayne - see map. (J.H.Aston)

6. Following transfer of the lines to the Western Region, ex-GWR 6400 class 0-6-0PTs were introduced to the branch in May 1963, along with push-pull coaches of the same origin. No.6430 is seen propelling the 5.31pm departure on 22nd May 1963. (J.H.Aston)

Seaton Junction	1928	1936
Number of passenger tickets issued	11740	8919
Number of season tickets issued	28	42
Number of tickets collected	14397	10916
Number of telegrams	4268	3046
Parcels forwarded	1381	1057
Parcels received	1836	1912
Horses forwarded	8	18
Cans of milk forwarded	16141	1267144
Cans of milk received	49	30816
General goods forwarded (tons)	341	654
General goods received (tons)	496	550
Coal, coke etc. received (tons)	170	550
Other minerals forwarded (tons)	-	6
Other minerals received (tons)	1242	123
Trucks livestock forwarded	25	-
Trucks livestock received	17	-
Lavatory pennies	1152	1764

7. Class S15 no.30845 heads a freight train on the down through road. For many years there were three through goods trains, in addition to the local service and milk trains from the Express Dairy depot on the right. No.34081 *92 Squadron* has called with the 9.35am Exeter Central all stations to Templecombe on 22nd May 1963. The timetable footnote read "Through carriage to Waterloo, arr 2.15pm". The branch signals are on the left. (J.H.Aston)

8. DMUs displaced steam on the branch on 4th November 1963 but failed to effect sufficient economy to prevent closure. Note the milk tankers in the background and the distance of the canopy from the platform edge. The signal box was in use from 3rd April 1928 until 11th June 1967. (Lens of Sutton)

9. Owing to failures of the DMUs in February 1965, steam returned to the branch in the form of 1400 class 0-4-2Ts. No.1450 also saw service at this period. A "Warship" diesel is visible on the main line, this class having been introduced to the route in 1964. (C.L.Caddy)

10. Passenger services were withdrawn from the station and branch on 7th March 1966. The goods yard closed on 18th April 1966 but coal traffic continued until 8th May 1967 and milk for a little longer. A photograph of no.50009 *Conqueror* on 10th August 1990 shows that both platforms, the up canopy and building and both footbridges remained, the cameraman being on the public one. The main line was singled on 11th June 1967. (C.Wilson)

This junction is also featured in our *Yeovil to Exeter* **album, pictures numbers 46 to 54.**

SOUTH OF SEATON JUNCTION

11. One of the trio of Lyme Regis engines, no.30584, is seen with the 10.10am Seaton to Waterloo train on 18th June 1949. The 0415 class only worked this one train on summer Saturdays - in the following years, one of them was rostered for the 2.40pm departure instead, but otherwise they did not work the branch regularly. (S.C.Nash)

12. Class M7 no.30046 has a clear exhaust as it runs north from Colyton on 24th May 1957, its gentle clatter leaving the hens to range freely and undisturbed. Mixed trains were shown in the timetables from the earliest days. (T.Wright)

13. A westward view indicates the relationship between the station and the picturesque town, which were separated by the flood plain of the River Coly. The winding narrow streets have great charm, as has the church with its square tower surmounted by an octagon. (Lens of Sutton)

The 1904 survey shows how the station was built on a shelf on the side of the valley. It was "Colyton Town" from March 1868 until September 1890.

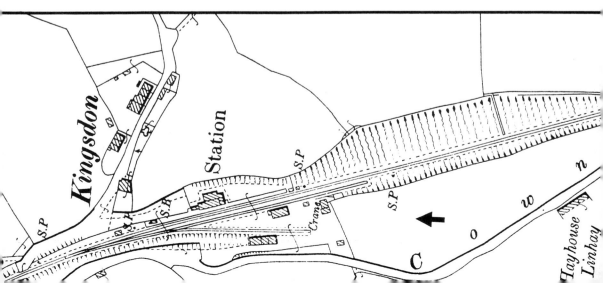

14. Included in this undated picture is a new signal ready for commissioning and a 5-ton crane. The water tank was added in 1873. (Lens of Sutton)

Colyton	1928	1936
Number of passenger tickets issued	19814	13431
Number of season tickets issued	23	54
Number of tickets collected	27331	15398
Number of telegrams	645	-
Parcels forwarded	1009	1097
Parcels received	5553	6036
Cans of milk forwarded	4226	-
Cans of milk received	13	-
General goods forwarded (tons)	626	265
General goods received (tons)	4015	3864
Coal, coke etc. received (tons)	2712	2736
Other minerals forwarded (tons)	4	-
Other minerals received (tons)	3282	174
Trucks livestock forwarded	26	14
Trucks livestock received	11	1
Lavatory pennies	168	101

15. Vans stand in the platform while coaches enter the sidings, the reverse of normal mixed train operation. The coaches would have been empty and might have been stabled here if Seaton was suffering congestion with excursions. (Lens of Sutton)

16. The signal box ceased to be used regularly on 4th April 1922 but was used as a ground frame until 4th November 1958. On 17th June 1949, its roof ventilator door was hanging functionless as class M7 no.30055 propelled its train to Seaton - hence the tail lamp on the engine. (S.C.Nash)

17. No.30021 is propelling the 2.5pm from Seaton Junction on 2nd June 1959, but the driver is not visible at the controls. By that time, the goods shed had lost its canopy - compare with previous photographs. The water tank had gained a roof but lost its cladding. (J.H.Aston)

18. The demolition of the signal box resulted in a two-lever ground frame being provided (left) and the stone-quoined shed becoming more evident from this angle. It was probably used for passenger train parcels - the forerunner of Red Star. Ex-GWR no.6430 is seen with the 6.10pm from Seaton on 25th May 1963. (J.H.Aston)

19. The same locomotive was recorded six weeks later, this view revealing that both the station nameboard and the loading gauge were supported by redundant running rails. The oil lamp at least has an ornate post - the barley sugar design. (R.C.Riley)

20. Carpets and a carton await delivery as one of the recently introduced class 2s, no.41309, waits with the 10.30 from the Junction on 1st June 1963. The yard is well stocked with coal but it was closed on 3rd February 1964, station manning ceasing on the same day. (J.H.Aston)

21. The sidings were lifted in May 1964 but the rails were still awaiting collection as the LCGB railtour passed through on 7th March 1965. This class 4 2-6-4T was a Brighton product and is carrying the main line headcode. (S.C.Nash)

22. The station building is seen in the railless era, its round-headed windows and steeply pitched roof contrasting with the square panes and flat roof of the shed on the right. Goods outward had once included cowhides and wooden domestic appliances. (C.Hall)

23. The station reopened on 8th March 1980 although the old platform (right) would not be used directly by the passengers on the trams of the Seaton & District Tramway Company. This is the scene on the following day. (E.Wilmshurst)

25. The sun shades and white paving make a pleasant environment for tourists, even if they clash with the historic building. The Ruston class 48DL was acquired in May 1973 to help with the construction work. (P.G.Barnes)

24. A July 1990 view shows a tram arriving, having passed the old goods shed, then used by a firm of builders. The station buildings have survived and are in use as a shop and buffet. Two motor generators (one at the depot and one at Colyton) receive mains supply at 415 volts AC and produce traction current at 120 volts DC. The company also has two diesel powered generators for use at peak times. (P.G.Barnes)

SOUTH OF COLYTON

26. Excursions were operated to Seaton from a wide variety of places. This is from Yeovil Town on 16th June 1960, class U no. 31805 having run round its train at Seaton Junction. The next picture was taken 30 years later at the same location. (S.C.Nash)

27. Between Colyton and Colyford there are two passing loops with automatic points. This is the southern one at Tye Lane. Near the northern one at Cownhayne there is a request stop for local passengers. (P.G.Barnes)

COLYFORD

28. The barrow largely obscures the crossing cottage which was built in 1867 at a cost of £525. It included a booking office. On the right is a living van of the type used by steam roller drivers - less obvious is the 5-lever ground frame. (Lens of Sutton)

The 1904 map marks the position of the crossing cottage and the bridge over the River Coly.

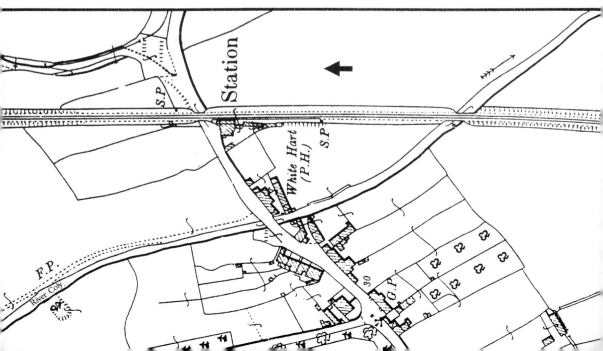

29. The cottage was demolished and replaced by a concrete slab wall, apparently used as a bicycle park. Beyond the wooden building is a cast iron urinal which remarkably is still standing today. The Axe Estuary is in the distance. In the summer of 1957 there would be about a dozen parcels or boxes of fish and around 20 passengers in a week. (Lens of Sutton)

Colyford	1928	1936
Number of passenger tickets issued	4968	2385
Number of season tickets issued	-	6
Number of tickets collected	4271	2414
Parcels forwarded	288	269
Parcels received	616	493
Cans of milk forwarded	579	2126

30. A pre-cast concrete building was eventually provided but oil lighting continued. The gradient post shows that no.30045 is leaving the flat tidal valley - note the pump on its smokebox, which provided compressed air for the push-pull mechanism. (P.Hay)

31. A second photograph from August 1959 includes the ground frame, which had two levers by then, as the signals had gone. Hanging flower baskets give cheer to the concrete structures. No. 30021 is displaying the headcode for Exeter Central to Sidmouth! (T.Wright)

32. Class 2 2-6-2T no. 41309 arrives with two ex-GWR autocoaches on 1st June 1963, bearing the main line headcode. Only single shift staffing was provided and so the guard had to open and close the gates at other times. (J.H.Aston)

33. DMUs were obliged to carry tail lamps, even in daylight, to indicate their integrity. This is 12th September 1964. During the winter a single car was more than adequate. (C.L.Caddy)

34. A northward view at Easter 1973 shows the old level crossing gates still in place. Trams did not cross the main road until 1980, following the installation of driver-operated flashing lights. Ex-Sheffield grooved rails were laid across the highway on the night of 15th November 1976. The old platform was bulldozed into a heap on the right. (K.Thorpe coll.)

35. Swan's Nest Loop and Axmouth Loop are south of Colyford, on the banks of the River Axe - an area popular with ornithologists. This is Swans Nest. No. 8 had been built in 1967, and was one of six cars to have been moved by the company from Eastbourne when the Crumbles line closed in 1969 - see pictures 40 - 45 in our *Eastbourne to Hastings* album. (E.Wilmshurst)

36. Seaton is in the background, as 1963-built no. 2 rattles north in July 1990 and approaches Axmouth Loop. Based on the Metropolitan Electric Tramway's design, this vehicle is red and cream, with gold lining. All the equipment was regauged from 2ft to 2ft 9ins when moved from Eastbourne. (P.G.Barnes)

SEATON TRAMWAY DEPOT

37. Southbound on 3rd July 1990, car no. 6 waits in Riverside Loop, the river being visible on the right. The points in the foreground give access to the depot. (P.G.Barnes)

38. A few seconds later, no. 6 leaves the loop and is about to turn sharply to the right on the first of four right angled bends which take the line round the boundary of the holiday camp to the terminus. (P.G.Barnes)

39. The depot was built at the northern limit of the former station site and is seen on 22nd October 1972, prior to the completion of overhead wiring. Until 23rd September 1973, all trams were accompanied by a battery truck (left), the cable from the trolley head being connected to it. No. 12 was later converted to a double-decker. (C.L.Caddy)

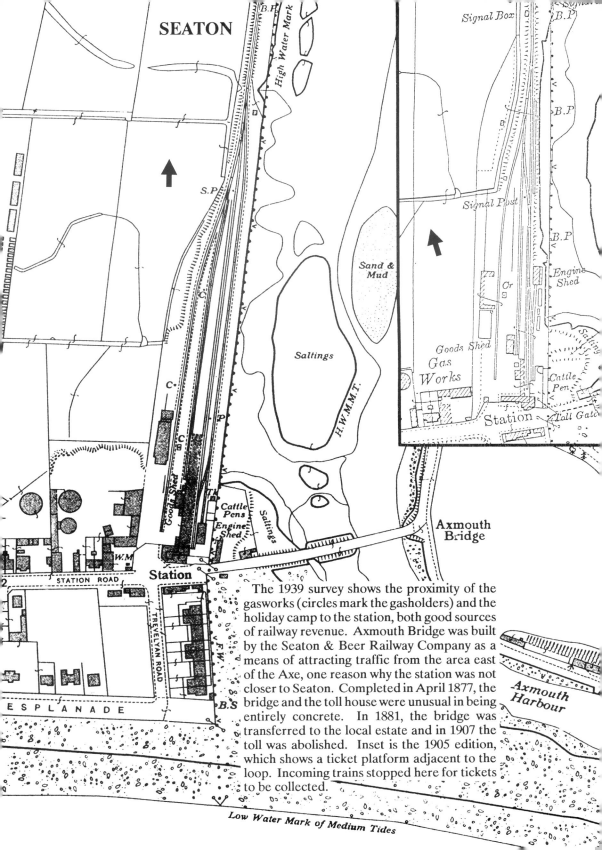

SEATON

High Water Mark

S.P.

Signal Box

B.P

Signal Post

B.P

B.P

Sand & Mud

Engine Shed

Cr

Saltings

H.W.M.M.T.

Goods Shed

Gas Works

Cattle Pen

C.

C.

Station

Toll Gate

C

P

Goods Shed

Cattle Pens

Saltings

T.H

Engine Shed

Axmouth Bridge

W.M

STATION ROAD

Station

TREVELYAN ROAD

F.W.

B.S

ESPLANADE

Axmouth Harbour

The 1939 survey shows the proximity of the gasworks (circles mark the gasholders) and the holiday camp to the station, both good sources of railway revenue. Axmouth Bridge was built by the Seaton & Beer Railway Company as a means of attracting traffic from the area east of the Axe, one reason why the station was not closer to Seaton. Completed in April 1877, the bridge and the toll house were unusual in being entirely concrete. In 1881, the bridge was transferred to the local estate and in 1907 the toll was abolished. Inset is the 1905 edition, which shows a ticket platform adjacent to the loop. Incoming trains stopped here for tickets to be collected.

Low Water Mark of Medium Tides

40. Although built by the S&BR, the design of the buildings included the round-headed windows typical of so many LSWR stations. Generous provision was made for the station master and his family in the double-storeyed part. (Lens of Sutton)

42. There was no run round facility at the platform, trains having to reverse up the main line until the advent of push-pull units. Southsea, Ilfracombe and Paris are among the destinations being promoted. (Lens of Sutton)

41. Initially the main platform was so short that it had to be extended within a year of the opening. The shorter of the two platforms is on the right and a van stands at the end loading dock on the left. (Lens of Sutton)

43. No. B214 was another ex-LBSCR
locomotive allocated to the branch in June
1930, many of these class D1s having been
made redundant by electrification. Near the
chimney can be seen the water tank level
gauge, the pointer at the bottom of the scale
indicating that the water was at the top of the
tank. (Lens of Sutton)

Seaton	1928	1936
Number of passenger tickets issued	25059	13471
Number of season tickets issued	60	183
Number of tickets collected	65533	45081
Number of telegrams	1339	1475
Parcels forwarded	3401	2412
Parcels received	20582	21994
Horses forwarded	7	5
Cans of milk forwarded	96	3923
Cans of milk received	353	3753
General goods forwarded (tons)	668	423
General goods received (tons)	2746	1929
Coal, coke etc. received (tons)	5007	5832
Other minerals forwarded (tons)	629	65
Other minerals received (tons)	4582	1095
Trucks livestock forwarded	8	13
Trucks livestock received	106	16
Lavatory pennies	1920	3492

44. The engine shed is in the background as class O2 no. E187 waits to depart. Built in 1890, this engine received the E prefix (Eastleigh) in 1923 and lost it in 1932. Two of this class displaced the D1s in 1932 and were in turn superseded by M7s after a few years. (Lens of Sutton)

45. Class O2 no. 207 was fitted with compressed air equipment in September 1933 for push-pull working of the branch. Sister engine no. 187 had been similarly treated in the previous year. The coach is ex-LSWR gated stock, which had trellis sliding gates at the vestibule. (Lens of Sutton)

46. The timber built engine shed had been erected at a cost of £200 before the line opened, but by the 1930s it needed props on the estuary side. The low short platforms restricted the growth of traffic, as did the cramped track layout. (Lens of Sutton)

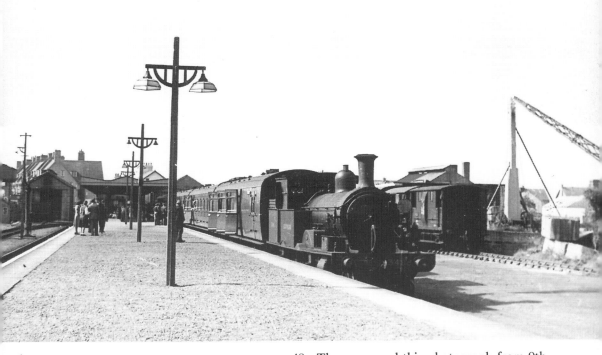

47. Even the engine shed was cramped and a potential danger to enginemen. This northward view includes the coaling stage, the original signal box, the low short platforms and the loop. All these were swept away during 1935-36, although the box had only been used at peak times since 11th January 1930, when a ground frame had been installed at the south end of the platform for normal use. (Lens of Sutton)

48. The maps and this photograph from 9th July 1945 show that the platforms and the tracks were greatly lengthened. A locomotive shed was built (left). On the right is the roof of the gasworks and limestone blocks in the yard of the Beer Stone Company. Class 0415 4-4-2T no. 3488 waits with 10.10am Saturday through coaches to Waterloo. (H.C.Casserley)

49. Concrete was used for the new coaling stage and tank supports, the latter being footbridge components. Unusually, cattle pens were placed between the coal and the locomotive shed. Goods outward included pebbles from the beach. (Lens of Sutton)

50. Another unusual feature was the siting of the new 20-lever signal box next to the buffers. The reason was that the signalman could be employed more easily on station duties between trains. It was brought into use on 28th June 1936. (Lens of Sutton)

51. The signal box is partially visible on the left. The single coach on the right is probably destined for Waterloo and will be attached to the next local train to the junction. There was ample space to handle the crowds of holidaymakers at peak periods. (Lens of Sutton)

52. At peak times, the goods yard would be crammed with coaches, the wagons being stabled at other stations for the weekend. The locomotive siding would be busy with visiting main line locomotives. Examples on 6th June 1960 were U class no. 31805 and "West Country" class no. 34096 *Trevone*. (S.C.Nash)

53. On 1st June 1963, the branch was worked by BR class 2 no. 41309, a locomotive type used for a limited period. The coaches are fitted with ground level steps which were at one time swung out for passengers at rural locations on the GWR. (J.H.Aston)

54. On 17th August 1963 no. 6412 had been working the branch push-pull train. Meanwhile SR Mogul no. 31632 had just arrived with the Seaton through coaches off the 9.0am from Waterloo. Both locos then double-headed the 1.26pm branch train back to the Junction. (J.N.Faulkner)

55. No. 6412 is seen again on 26th October 1963, by which time the crowds had disappeared. On the left is the signal box, which closed on 2nd May 1965 when all points were taken out of use and only one DMU worked the branch. (E.Wilmshurst)

56. Three photographs from 13th March 1965 show the station in its last complete year of operation. The newly designed BR logo is clear but the white flagpole is less so, blending too closely with the background. (C.L.Caddy)

57. The goods shed (partly hidden by the signal box) had an external siding, as at Colyton, but lost this in 1936 - see maps. The goods yard closed on 3rd February 1964 but the siding and coal staithes remained. The site is now occupied by the Racal Electronics factory (C.L.Caddy)

58. The concrete nameboard posts, the lamp posts and the platform slabs had all been produced at the SR Concrete Works at Exmouth Junction. Only the few posts near the hut remain today and can be seen in picture no. 38. (C.L.Caddy)

59. The engine shed closed on 4th November 1963 having been built of Muribloc in 1937. A single railcar saw out the final months of this once busy branch. (Lens of Sutton)

SEATON TRAMWAY TERMINUS

60. The half-mile extension from the depot to the main town car park was opened on 17th May 1975. This involved the extension of the former railway embankment on a gradient of 1 in 40 to take the tramway to ground level and the construction of a bridge over a stream, using steel from the former station canopy. This and the next two pictures were taken in 1980. (T.Wright)

61. No. 01 is a mobile shop which is hauled to and from the depot each day. Other unusual cars include no. 4, a Blackpool style "boat car", and no. 14, a single deck saloon tram built from components of a full size MET car, no. 94. A regular service is provided throughout the year, except at weekends in the winter. (T.Wright)

62. The terminus is much closer to the town centre than was the former station and is situated in an unbelievably boring public car park, totally devoid of trees, furniture or any features to break the expanse of tarmac. A vintage Bedford OB coach added interest, however, on 9th March 1980. (E.Wilmshurst)

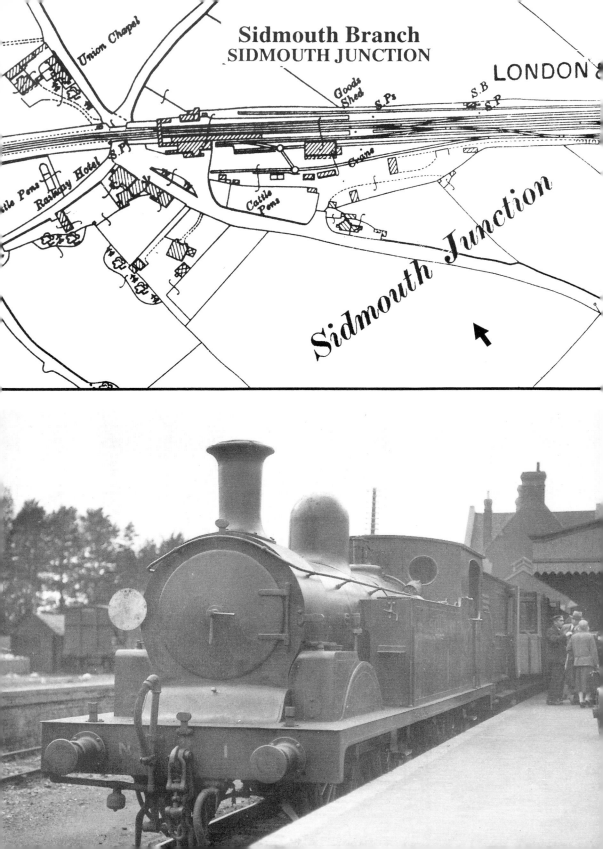

Sidmouth Branch
SIDMOUTH JUNCTION

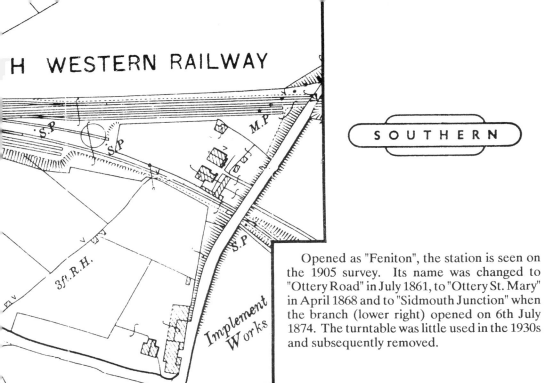

H WESTERN RAILWAY

SOUTHERN

Opened as "Feniton", the station is seen on the 1905 survey. Its name was changed to "Ottery Road" in July 1861, to "Ottery St. Mary" in April 1868 and to "Sidmouth Junction" when the branch (lower right) opened on 6th July 1874. The turntable was little used in the 1930s and subsequently removed.

63. Most trains for the branch started from the bay platform - class T1 no. 1 is about to do so on 12th June 1926. The dock on the left also had an end-loading facility, used for such items as agricultural equipment and the carriages of the gentry. (H.C.Casserley)

64. On a peaceful Sunday afternoon in August 1938, class M7 0-4-4T no. 377 is departing for Sidmouth, having just run round its train, the 2.55pm from Axminster. It is about to pass under a road bridge which is still standing. (J.R.W.Kirkby)

65. The 9.3am from Honiton on 15th June 1949 arrived at Sidmouth Junction at 9.12. Nos 49 and 245 have just run round their train and are about to leave at 9.25 with coaches for Sidmouth and Exmouth, the train dividing at Tipton St. Johns. This service operated on Mondays to Fridays. (S.C.Nash)

66. Double heading to Tipton St. Johns was not uncommon. Here we witness nos. 30124 and 30133 departing at 3.2pm with the 12 coaches of the 11.35am from Waterloo on 17th June 1950. Partially obscured by the third coach, the 31-lever signal box was functional until 21st May 1967. (J.J.Smith)

67. No. 35025 *Brocklebank Line* collects the coaches of the 9.52am from Exmouth and the 10.30 from Sidmouth on 31st May 1963. It will attach them to the 8.10 from Ilfracombe (right) which it had brought on from Exeter Central. The combined train was due at Waterloo at 2.15 pm. On the left, class 2 2-6-2T no. 41318 waits with the 10.55 to Sidmouth on 31st May 1963. (J.H.Aston)

68. Passengers wait on the down platform on 17th August 1963 for the 2.22pm from Sidmouth, which will be attached to the 11.48am Plymouth to Waterloo train. Beyond the crossing is the ground frame box, which was in use until 23rd June 1974. The station master's office was in the nearest part of the up side building. (J.N.Faulkner)

69. The 14.10 Exeter St. David's to Waterloo on 14th September 1966 was hauled by no. D820 *Grenville*, one of the "Warship" class introduced to the route in 1964. In the bay is the 14.55 to Sidmouth. Goods facilities were withdrawn on 6th September 1965. (J.M.Tolson/F.Hornby)

70. The junction and the branch both closed to passengers on 6th March 1967 and the main line was singled on 11th June following. The down platform was reopened as "Feniton" on 3rd May 1971, the 1860 buildings being demolished to make way for a prefabricated booking office, erected in 1974. (C.L.Caddy)

Other Views of this junction can be found in the companion album, *Yeovil to Exeter*, **pictures 64 to 72.**

OTTERY ST. MARY

Ottery St. Mary	1928	1936
Number of passenger tickets issued	20190	9601
Number of season tickets issued	101	113
Number of tickets collected	29027	17360
Number of telegrams	743	-
Parcels forwarded	2419	1304
Parcels received	5862	7452
Horses forwarded	25	6
Cans of milk forwarded	356	-
General goods forwarded (tons)	1317	468
General goods received (tons)	4398	5089
Coal, coke etc. received (tons)	4343	4370
Other minerals forwarded (tons)	1248	60
Other minerals received (tons)	2064	345
Trucks livestock forwarded	156	153
Trucks livestock received	50	12
Lavatory pennies	408	642

The 1905 edition has the single line from Sidmouth Junction on the left and the headshunt parallel to it. The crane was of 2-ton lifting capacity. Note the convenient proximity of the gasworks to the sidings.

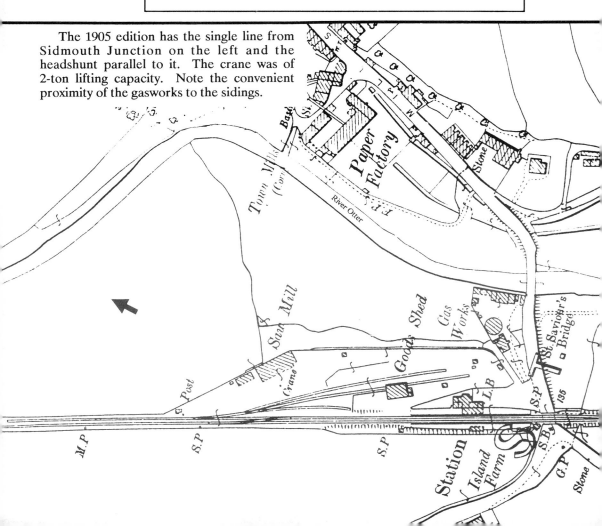

71. Situated ½ mile west of the town centre, the station was at the bottom of the Otter Valley. This view from West Hill has the bridge over the River Otter in the centre foreground, the signal box on the left, the station right of centre and the goods shed on the right. (Lens of Sutton)

72. Four members of staff are ready for action as class T1 0-4-4T no. 362 arrives from the junction. The locomotive has its original Adams-style chimney and beyond it is the chimney of the sawmill. (Lens of Sutton)

73. An up train passes over the level crossing to collect the well dressed crowd, every lady with a fashionable wide-brimmed hat. The population of the town remained little changed at about 4000 throughout the 93 years it was served by the railway. (Lens of Sutton)

74. A spacious approach was provided but when photographed in September 1963 its use was in decline. Unlike the Seaton branch, wagons could pass through the goods shed. A van has done so on the right. (R.M.Casserley)

75. This signal box came into use on 20th November 1955, replacing a smaller structure on the other side of the track. Small 5-lever crossing boxes were situated at Gosford Gates, 1½ miles to the north, and at Cadhay Gates, ½ mile north. (Lens of Sutton)

76. On 7th March 1965, the Locomotive Club of Great Britain visited the branch for the second time - a repeat of the tour run a week earlier. The train left Waterloo at 9.02am and half the party visited the Lyme Regis branch. The train was seen earlier in picture no. 21. (S.C.Nash)

77. The loop had been extended about 50 yards at its southern end on 22nd November 1936, in order to accommodate the longer holiday trains. The lever frame was against the back wall - a departure from tradition. (C.L.Caddy)

78. The goods shed was still standing in 1991, although much neglected. Goods traffic ceased on 6th September 1965, although coal was still handled until 8th May 1967, eight weeks after passenger services ceased. Latterly the shed has been used by the sawmill. (M.Turvey)

79. An April 1991 photograph shows that the main building and the goods shed were still extant. The mural is on that part occupied by Devon County Council's Youth Centre. (V.Mitchell)

80. Two miles south of the station and ¼ mile north of Tipton St. Johns, the line crossed the 55yd long Ottery St. Mary Viaduct. The substantial structure was still standing in 1991. (M.Turvey)

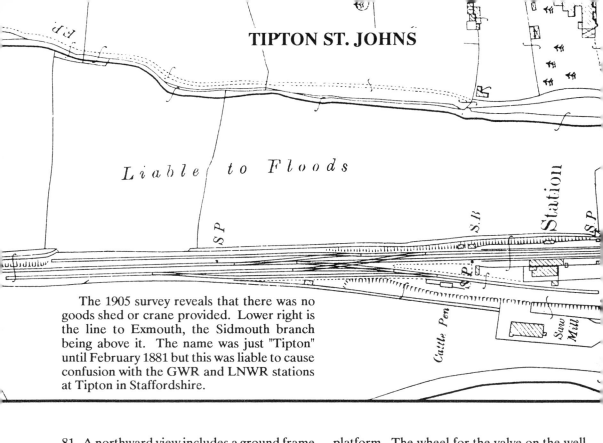

TIPTON ST. JOHNS

Liable to Floods

The 1905 survey reveals that there was no goods shed or crane provided. Lower right is the line to Exmouth, the Sidmouth branch being above it. The name was just "Tipton" until February 1881 but this was liable to cause confusion with the GWR and LNWR stations at Tipton in Staffordshire.

81. A northward view includes a ground frame beyond the end of the down platform and signals which allowed trains to arrive at either platform. The wheel for the valve on the well insulated water column was on the far side of it. (Lens of Sutton)

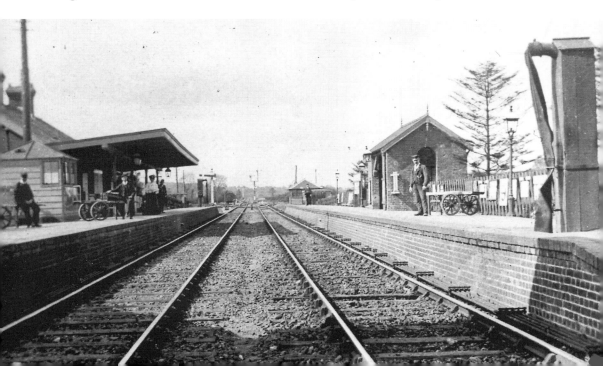

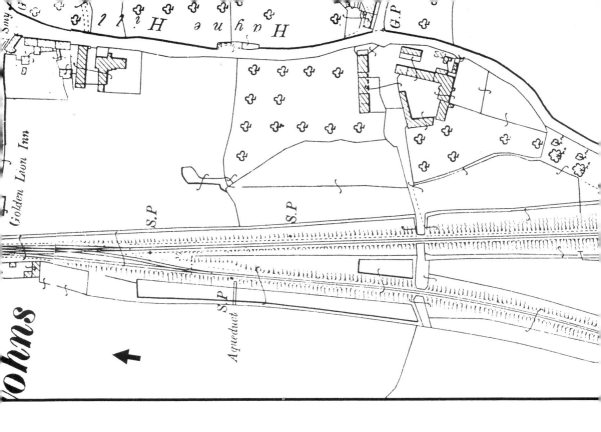

82. The signal box had 33 levers and a gate wheel. It was commissioned in March 1897, in readiness for the opening of the line to Budleigh Salterton on 15th May of that year. Its predecessor was on the opposite side of the track and the road. (Lens of Sutton)

84. The two coaches for Sidmouth leave behind class M7 no.245 on 15th June 1949. The Exmouth portion remains in the platform awaiting its locomotive which is standing to the left of the photographer. This is the train seen earlier, in picture no. 65. (S.C.Nash)

83. Seen on 18th June 1926, class T1 no. 1 waits to leave for Sidmouth Junction. Note that the down signals had been altered by then, preventing down trains entering the up platform. (H.C.Casserley)

CAMPING COACHES

All the fun of a camping holiday without any of the bother! A camping coach is a corridor railway carriage converted to form a delightful summer home for six people. The internal fittings have been removed to provide in a compact layout a dining and living room, a kitchen, and three bedrooms each accommodating two persons in full-length beds or bunks.

The kitchen is well equipped. All bed and table linen, crockery and cutlery is provided.

The coaches may be booked for one or two weeks, from 2.0 p.m. Saturday to 12 noon on the following Saturday or Saturday week from the end of March to mid-October.

Other than the actual rental, the only condition attaching to this singularly carefree holiday is that not less than the equivalent of four adult ordinary return rail tickets are purchased between your home station and the station where the camping coach is situated.

Oil for cooking and lighting can be purchased from the station-master and clean linen is provided each week.

85. Visible on the left of the previous picture is camping coach no. 13, formerly LSWR no. 5019. A holiday at the end of the coal siding would cost a family of six £9 for a week in the summer of 1955. Such coaches were taken away for servicing during the winter. (J.H.Aston)

86. The footbridge was added in February 1898 at the insistence of the Railway Inspectorate, who deemed it necessary at a junction station. Class M7 no. 30670 is taking water from the brazier-equipped water column on 19th August 1951. (N.Sprinks)

87. No. 30669 waits for no. 30670 to clear the single line from Ottery St. Mary on 17th August 1953. By then the up starting signal was mounted on a concrete post instead of the wooden one seen earlier. It is evident that the up sidings included a loop in which terminating branch trains could run round clear of the running lines. (N.L.Browne)

BETWEEN TIPTON ST. JOHN'S AND SIDMOUTH.

Loads of trains.—The maximum loads of trains worked by one engine between Tipton St. John's and Sidmouth stations are as follows :—

Down trains from Tipton St. John's to Sidmouth.			Up trains from Sidmouth to Tipton St. John's.		
Passenger.—O.2 class engines, 128 tons	T.1 class engines. 150 tons	M.7 class engines. 160 tons	**Passenger.**—O.2 class engines. 150 tons	T.1 class engines. 170 tons	M.7 class engines. 180 tons
Goods.—Not exceeding equal to 16 loaded goods wagons and 1 heavy van or 2 light vans.			**Goods.**—Not exceeding equal to 23 loaded goods wagons and 1 heavy van or 2 light vans with a Guard in each.		
Mixed.—64 tons, equal to 6 loaded goods wagons, and one brake van.			**Mixed.**—64 tons, equal to 6 loaded goods wagons, and one brake van.		

A goods train run between Tipton St. John's and Sidmouth must have at the rear a heavy brake van of not less than 20 tons, which, whenever possible, should be a van fitted with sanding apparatus. Should, however, a brake van of this description not be obtainable, two smaller brake vans, with a man in each must be provided at the rear.

The Station Masters at Sidmouth Junction, Tipton St. John's and Sidmouth will be responsible for seeing that these instructions are obeyed.

Not more than one coach conveying passengers, or two horse boxes, P.L. vans, empty coaches, etc., may be attached outside the rear brake in either direction between Tipton St. John's and Sidmouth, and no vehicle must be so attached unless fitted with the vacuum brake complete.

88. The water tank stood on the site of the first signal box. No.82011 passes it on 3rd August 1959, having just descended the 1 in 45 gradient with the 10.20am Sidmouth-Waterloo coaches. A few minutes earlier no.82024 had brought in the coaches from Exmouth, has run round them, and is waiting in the distance to propel them back into the station where both portions would be connected. (S.C.Nash)

89. Beyond the DMU, catch points are visible at the foot of the incline.   These were to prevent any runaways crossing the road and entering the station.   The 16.05 Exeter-Sidmouth service is arriving on 13th September 1966, having reversed at Exmouth. (J.M.Tolson/F.Hornby)

Tipton St. Johns	1928	1936
Number of passenger tickets issued	10524	5014
Number of season tickets issued	16	39
Number of tickets collected	10480	6154
Number of telegrams	1266	405
Parcels forwarded	1433	442
Parcels received	406	590
Horses forwarded	9	11
Cans of milk forwarded	2425	8519
Cans of milk received	23	-
General goods forwarded (tons)	177	69
General goods received (tons)	1033	851
Coal, coke etc. received (tons)	397	237
Other minerals forwarded (tons)	-	100
Other minerals received (tons)	100	7
Trucks livestock forwarded	8	7
Trucks livestock received	27	-
Lavatory pennies	97	235

90. The 15.02 Sidmouth to Exeter service is seen on the following day. Two reversals on this short journey were accomplished with little effort using DMUs. The siding loop in the background was no longer needed. Goods facilities had been withdrawn on 27th January 1964. (J.M.Tolson/F.Hornby)

91. The main building was still standing in 1991, in use as a private house. It is seen from the site of the level crossing where some gate-posts remain in place. (M.Turvey)

SOUTH OF TIPTON ST. JOHNS

92.   Although not sharp, this picture does show the original track arrangements. The diamond crossing was later abandoned in favour of the layout seen in the photographs. Note the absence of catch points, not added until 1953. (Lens of Sutton)

93.   Venn Ottery church and the Exmouth branch bridge over the River Otter are included in this picture of class M7 no. 30374 starting the two-mile climb at 1 in 45 on 15th June 1949. Trains of up to 16 wagons (the maximum) were required to have a 20 ton brake van or two smaller ones, both manned. (S.C.Nash)

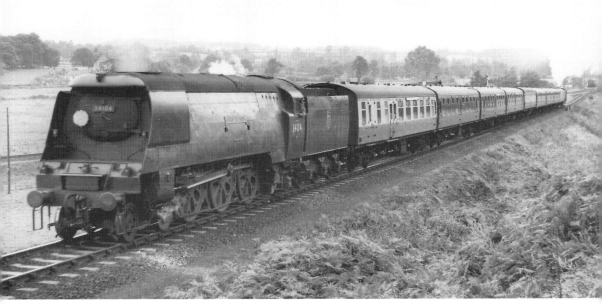

94. Down passenger trains were limited to 160 tons unassisted, and so no. 34104 *Bere Alston* was being helped at the rear by class 2 2-6-2T no. 82017 on 3rd August 1959, the train being a Plymouth - Sidmouth excursion. (S.C.Nash)

95. Descending at 1 in 54, no. 30374 is one mile from Sidmouth on 15th June 1949. The train is part of the 10.50am from Waterloo - 2.17pm from Sidmouth Junction. (S.C.Nash)

SIDMOUTH

The 1905 survey includes the locomotive water supply (marked reservoir) but omits the crossovers evident in the photographs.

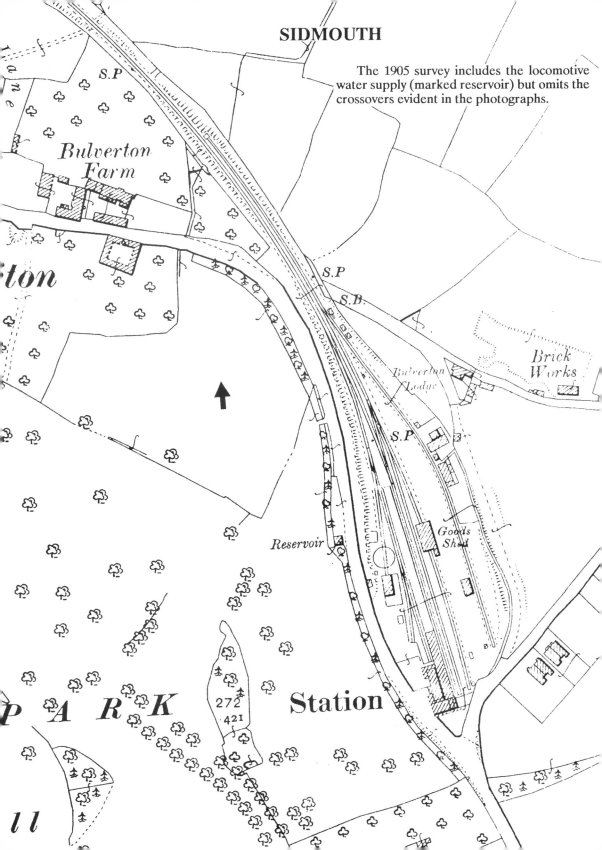

S.P

Bulverton Farm

ton

S.P

S.B.

Brick Works

Bulverton Lodge

S.P

Goods Shed

Reservoir

P A R K

272
421

Station

l l

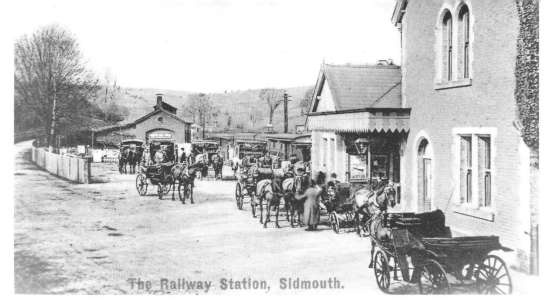

The Railway Station, Sidmouth.

96. With the station being 200 ft above sea level and nearly one mile from the town centre, road transport was popular, as illustrated by this Edwardian postcard. (Lens of Sutton)

SIDMOUTH.
ROYAL YORK HOTEL
CENTRE OF ESPLANADE.
OLD ESTABLISHED. Facing South. Finest position—
Warm and Sunny. New South Lounge added. Appointed
A.A. and R.A.C. Near Brine Baths. Golf. Cricket. Billiards.
Garage Free. Moderate Terms. Telephone: 43.
Telegrams: "York, Sidmouth."
Resident Proprietors—**Mr. and Mrs. MITCHELL.**
(Also the LONDON HOTEL.)

97. A busy goods yard forms the backdrop to this picture of class T1 no.11 standing in front of the turntable and adjacent to the coal stage. Seen with its original cast stovepipe chimney, no. 11 was in use from 1895 until 1944. (Lens of Sutton)

98. The flanged Drummond-style chimney indicates a later date but the coaches are still short, probably four-wheelers. This is another undated postcard view. (Lens of Sutton)

99. Bogie coaches stand in the shorter platform, their lavatory compartments suggesting that they were through coaches from London. The engine release crossover remained to the end, but the less obvious goods crossover (lower left) was removed in the 1930s. (Lens of Sutton)

100. Through coaches are stabled on the right while class T1 no. E80 waits with compartment stock on 4th August 1928. The canopy was extended towards the camera in 1935, as holiday crowds began to increase. (H.C.Casserley)

101. The first engine shed was of timber construction and was destroyed by fire on 7th January 1900. This is the replacement brick structure which remained in use until the mid-1930s, after which time locomotives were sent from Exmouth Junction. (Lens of Sutton)

102. Class M7 no. 668 runs round its train on 24th June 1938, prior to departure at 8.32am. Note that the non-passenger line has two-bolt fishplates, which allowed the sleepers to be placed closer together. (F.E.Box/NRM)

103. Transport to the town in 1948 was provided by a Devon General Bedford WLG. No. M419 stands outside the station master's front door on 28th June 1948. The bus was built in 1938 with a Birch body and withdrawn in 1951. (J.H.Aston)

104. *Bere Alston* shunts part of a Plymouth excursion on 3rd August 1959, the complete train having been seen in picture no. 94. The banking engine will have removed the other part of it onto the adjacent line. (S.C.Nash)

105. The signal box had 23 levers and was in use until the line closed. Class 2 2-6-2T no. 82010 arrives with an SR Maunsell corridor brake and a BR compartment coach on 13th October 1959. (R.C.Riley)

SIDMOUTH

106. No. 41306 is seen on 13th July 1960, shunting the private siding which is largely obscured by coaches in the previous picture. The vans conveyed Volkswagen vans from the importers at Ramsgate to the works of J.P. White, manufacturers of motor caravans. The siding was in use from 1958 until closure of the branch and was on the site of the former gasworks. (R.C.Riley)

107. Domestic fuel was still an important traffic when this photograph was taken in July 1960 but coal for the nearby gasworks had ceased to be carried by then. The Ford 8 probably belonged to the signalman. For many years the freight train left Sidmouth Junction at 7.20am and returned from Sidmouth at 3.5pm. (R.C.Riley)

SIDMOUTH.

Shunting.—When an empty coaching stock train is propelled by the engine from either of the platf lines to the single line in the direction of Tipton St. John's for the purpose of gravitating back into station, it must be accompanied by the Guard (who must ride in the brake van nearest the engine) a Shunter. The Shunter must not uncouple the engine until the train has come to rest on the single l and he has received an assurance from the Guard that the brake has been applied and the coaches under control ; and the Guard must not allow the coaches to commence running back into the stat until the engine has been shunted clear of the running line and the proper ground signal has been lowe for the movement to be made.

108. This and the next three pictures were taken on 13th July 1960 to give a complete pictorial survey of this almost unchanged Victorian terminus. One notable improvement evident here is the lengthened canopy.

Coaches standing in four different roads emphasise the difficulty of operating the cramped layout which could not easily be extended, as at Seaton. (R.C.Riley)

109. In addition to coal, the yard handled building materials, agricultural requirements and general merchandise. The jib of the 2-ton crane can be seen inside the goods shed. The fact that fuel is being hand pumped into the delivery van shows that the railway preferred to be independent of local suppliers. (R.C.Riley)

111. The 1900 locomotive shed ceased to be used in the mid-1930s, surprising in view of the fact that the nearby branches at Exmouth, Seaton and Lyme Regis retained functional sheds until the end of steam 30 years later. (R.C.Riley)

110. The Royal Mail van on the pavement is a reminder of a once important traffic on passenger trains. The motor cycle was a popular form of staff transport in this era and a distinct improvement on a bicycle in undulating Devon. (R.C.Riley)

SIDMOUTH JUNCTION, SIDMOUTH and EXMOUTH.—Southern.

Miles	Down. Week Days only.	mrn	mrn	mrn	mrn	mrn	mrn		aft	aft	aft	mrn	non	aft	aft	aft	aft	aft	aft	aft	aft	aft	
	162 London (W'loo) dep.	....	....	....	....	....	....	....	9 0	....	....	11 0	12 0	....	....	1 0	....	3 0	....	....	....	....	....
—	Sidmouth Junction dep.	....	....	8 4	8 41	9 33	11 7	....	1235	....	2 0	2 42	3 41	3 48	4 25	5 15	5 42	6 55	7 52	8 30	....	....	....
2¼	Ottery St. Mary	....	....	8 10	8 47	9 39	1113	....	1241	....	2 6	2 48	....	3 54	4 31	5 21	5 48	7 1	7 58	8 36	....	....	....
5	Tipton St. John's .. arr.	....	....	8 16	8 53	9 44	1121	....	1247	....	2 11	2 53	....	3 59	4 37	5 26	5 53	7 6	8 3	8 41	....	....	....
—	Tipton St. John's dep.	7 25	....	8 18	8 57	9 46	1124	....	1250	....	2 13	2 54	....	....	4 41	5 28	5 56	7 11	8 5	8 45	....	....	....
8½	Sidmouth .... arr.	7 35	....	8 23	9 7	9 56	1134	....	1 0	....	2 23	3 4	3 58	....	4 51	5 38	6 6	7 21	8 15	8 55	....	....	....
—	Tipton St. John's .. dep.	....	....	8 47	9 4	1023	1128	....	1253	....	....	....	....	4 1	4 46	....	6 0	7 16	....	8 50	....	....	....
6¾	Newton Poppleford	....	....	8 50	9 7	1026	1131	....	1256	....	....	....	....	....	4 49	....	6 3	7 19	....	8 53	....	....	....
9¾	East Budleigh	....	....	8 56	9 13	1032	1137	....	1 2	....	....	....	....	....	4 55	....	6 9	7 25	....	8 59	....	....	....
11¾	Budleigh Salterton	....	8 10	9 2	9 19	1038	1143	....	1 8	1 52	....	....	....	4 11	5 1	....	6 15	7 31	....	9 5	9 45	1030	....
14¾	Littleham	....	8 18	9 11	9 30	1050	1155	....	1 17	2 0	....	....	....	4 24	5 18	....	6 25	7 41	....	9 16	9 53	1038	....
16¾	Exmouth 168 ...... arr.	....	8 26	9 16	9 35	1055	12 0	....	1 22	2 5	....	....	....	4 29	5 26	....	6 31	7 47	....	9 22	9 58	1043	....

Miles	Up. Week Days only.	mrn	mrn	mrn	mrn	mrn	mrn	mrn		aft	aft	aft	aft	aft	aft	aft	aft	aft	aft	aft	aft	aft	
	Exmouth .... dep.	6 45	7 47	....	8 15	9 42	1020	1130	....	....	1 30	2 13	....	4 0	....	5 15	....	....	6 38	8 10	9 12	10 5	....
1¾	Littleham	6 50	7 52	....	8 20	9 47	1025	1135	....	....	1 35	2 18	....	4 5	....	5 20	....	....	6 43	8 15	9 17	1010	....
4¾	Budleigh Salterton	7 0	8 1	....	8 31	9 58	1040	1145	....	....	1 44	2 30	....	4 17	....	5 31	....	....	6 53	8 25	9 27	1019	....
7	East Budleigh	7 4	....	....	8 35	10 2	1044	1149	....	....	....	2 34	....	4 21	....	5 35	....	....	6 57	8 29	....	....	....
10	Newton Poppleford	7 10	....	....	8 41	10 8	1051	1155	....	....	....	2 40	....	4 27	....	5 41	....	....	7 3	8 35	....	....	....
11¾	Tipton St. John's .. arr.	7 15	....	....	8 46	1013	1056	12 0	....	....	....	2 45	....	4 32	....	5 46	....	....	7 8	8 40	....	....	....
—	Sidmouth .... dep.	7 10	....	8 30	8 45	1010	1055	1155	....	1 15	....	2 42	3 15	4 30	5 5	....	6 15	6 45	7 40	8 35	....	....	....
—	Tipton St. John's arr.	7 19	....	8 39	8 54	1019	11 4	12 4	....	1 24	....	2 51	3 24	4 39	5 14	....	6 24	6 54	7 49	8 44	....	....	....
—	Tipton St. John's .. dep.	7 22	....	....	8 58	1023	1110	12 6	....	1 26	....	3 1	3 26	4 43	5 16	....	6 26	6 56	7 53	8 46	....	....	....
13¾	Ottery St. Mary ... [163	7 26	....	....	9 2	1027	1114	1210	....	1 30	....	3 5	3 30	4 47	5 20	....	6 30	7 0	7 57	8 50	....	....	....
16¾	Sidmouth Jn. 162, arr.	7 36	....	....	9 12	1037	1124	1220	....	1 40	....	3 15	3 40	4 56	5 31	....	6 40	7 11	8 8	9 0	....	....	....
175¾	163 London (W'loo) arr.	1110	....	....	....	1 56	3 8	....	....	....	....	8 41	8 41	9 30	....	....	1120	....	3a58	....	....	....	....

a Via Eastleigh.

July 1924

112. A through train from Cleethorpes was introduced in 1960, running via Bath and Templecombe. It only operated for three summers and brought Eastern Region coaches to Sidmouth, seen in this and the previous picture. The journey took over ten hours. (Lens of Sutton)

THROUGH TRAIN SERVICE

BETWEEN

CLEETHORPES, GRIMSBY, LINCOLN, NOTTINGHAM, LEICESTER, BIRMINGHAM

AND

AXMINSTER (for Lyme Regis), SEATON JUNCTION (for Seaton), SIDMOUTH, BUDLEIGH SALTERTON, EXMOUTH

VIA BATH GREEN PARK AND TEMPLECOMBE

SATURDAYS ONLY

COMMENCES 1st JULY

From NORTH to SOUTH		From SOUTH to NORTH	
	am		am
Cleethorpes .. .. dep	7 0	Exmouth.. .. ..dep	10A42
Grimsby Docks .. .. ,,	7 8	Littleham .. .. ,,	10A47
Grimsby Town .. .. ,,	7 14	Budleigh Salterton .. .. ,,	10A55
Healing .. .. ,,	6b32	East Budleigh .. .. ,,	10 59
Habrough .. .. ,,	7 27	Sidmouth .. .. ,,	11A 7
Barnetby.. .. .. ,,	7 40	Tipton St. Johns .. .. ,,	11 16
Market Rasen .. .. ,,	8 0	Sidmouth Junction .. .. ,,	11 33
Lincoln (St. Mark's) .. .. .. ,,	8 27	Seaton .. .. ,,	11 7
Newark (Castle) .. .. ,,	8 53	Seaton Junction .. .. ,,	11 53
Fiskerton .. .. ,,	9 1	Lyme Regis .. .. ,,	11 8
Nottingham (Mid.) .. .. ,,	9 23		pm
Trent .. .. ,,	9 36	Axminster .. .. ,,	12 1
Loughborough (Mid.) .. .. .. ,,	9 49	Templecombe .. .. ,,	12 48
Leicester London Road .. .. .. ,,	10 10	Evercreech Junction .. .. .. ,,	1 10
Hinckley.. .. .. ,,	10 33	Bath Green Park .. .. ,,	2 18
Nuneaton Abbey Street .. .. .. ,,	10 43		
Birmingham New Street .. .. .. ,,	11 36	Gloucester Eastgate .. .. arr	3 16
	pm	Cheltenham Spa (Lansdown) .. .. ,,	4c20
Cheltenham Spa (Lansdown) .. .. ,,	12 47	Birmingham New Street .. .. .. ,,	4 44
Gloucester Eastgate .. .. ,,	1 5	Nuneaton Abbey Street .. .. .. ,,	5 26
		Hinckley.. .. .. ,,	5 37
Bath Green Park .. .. arr	2 2	Leicester London Road .. .. .. ,,	6 0
Evercreech Junction .. .. .. ,,	3 9	Loughborough (Mid.) .. .. .. ,,	6 24
Templecombe .. .. ,,	3 32	Trent .. .. ,,	6 36
Axminster .. .. ,,	4 21	Nottingham (Mid.) .. .. ,,	6 51
Lyme Regis .. .. ,,	5 3	Fiskerton .. .. ,,	7d30
Seaton Junction .. .. ,,	4 29	Newark (Castle) .. .. ,,	7 21
Seaton .. .. ,,	4 57	Lincoln (St. Mark's) .. .. .. ,,	7 53
Sidmouth Junction .. .. ,,	4 51	Market Rasen .. .. ,,	8 21
Tipton St. Johns .. .. ,,	5 5	Barnetby.. .. .. ,,	8 44
Sidmouth .. .. ,,	5 17	Habrough .. .. ,,	8 57
East Budleigh .. .. ,,	5 21	Healing .. .. ,,	9 6
Budleigh Salterton .. .. ,,	5 26	Grimsby Town .. .. ,,	9 13
Littleham .. .. ,,	5 35	Grimsby Docks .. .. ,,	9 20
Exmouth.. .. .. ,,	5 40	Cleethorpes .. .. ,,	9 31

A—Seats may be reserved at a fee of 2/– per seat upon personal or postal request to the Station Master. Early application is advisable

b—Change at Habrough

c—Change at Gloucester Eastgate

d—Change at Nottingham (Mid.)

LONDON to SALISBURY, YEOVIL, LYME REGIS, SEATON, SIDMOUTH, BUDLEIGH SALTERTON, EXMOUTH, OKEHAMPTON, TAVISTOCK & DEVONPORT

DOWN — MONDAYS TO FRIDAYS

		am	RC am	RC am	RC am	"ATLANTIC COAST EXPRESS" Commences 17th July	RC am	RC pm	RC pm	RB pm	RC pm	MB pm	RC pm	RC pm	RC pm
LONDON Waterloo	dep	1A10	9A 0		11A 0		11A 5	1A 0	3A 0		5 0		6A 0		7A 0
„ Paddington	„			9A30					1A30	3A30			5A50		
Salisbury	arr	2 57	10 50		12 23		12 32	2 39	4 41		7 0		7 45		8 25
Yeovil ⎰ Junction	„	4 49	11 52		1 59			3 43	5 55		8 14		8 48		9 15
⎱ Town	„	5 26	12 6		2 14			3 55	6 9		8 29		9 0		9 24
⎱ Pen Mill	„			12 31						4 26		6 1		9 23	
Lyme Regis	„	8Y 3	12 54		3J 9		2 8	4 57	7 8				10Y22		
Seaton	„	8 22	12 46		3J 5		2 15	4 57	7 15				10X18		10F 8
Sidmouth	„	8 29	1 18		2 13			5 30	6 44				10 10		
Budleigh Salterton	„	9 2	1 28		2 22			6 6	6 52				10 22		
Exmouth (via Tipton St. John's)	„		1 41		2 34				7 6				10 35		
Exmouth (via Exeter Central)	„	7 10						5 10							10 51
Okehampton	„	5 57	2 9		3J 8			5 40	7 27						11 17
Tavistock North	„	6 38	2 38		3J54		3 54	6 18	8 0						11 44
Devonport King's Road	„	7 23	3 9		4J20		4 20	6 48	8 27						12 13

DOWN — SATURDAYS

		15th July to 2nd September am	am	am	Runs 17th June to 1st July and 19th August to 2nd September	am	RC am	am	RC am	RC am	am	am	RB am	RC am	RC am	RC pm	15th July to 2nd September	pm	RC pm
LONDON Waterloo	dep	12AG15	1AD10		7 5	7A30		8A 3	8A22	8A54	9A 0		10A45	11A15	11A45	1A 0		1 5	
„ Paddington	„											9A40							1A30
Salisbury	arr	1650	2 57			9 10		9 47		9 58	1050		12 16	12 42	1 22	2 39		2 50	
Yeovil ⎰ Junction	„	4 17	4 59			10 8				12 0				1 33		3 41		3 58	
⎱ Town	„	4 29	5 26			10 24				12 13				1 44		3 55			
⎱ Pen Mill	„				1041						1232								4 29
Lyme Regis	„		8Y 3			12 0							2 16			5K 3		5 3	
Seaton	„		8H20			11 37		11 50		1 0			2 5			4K57		4 57	
Sidmouth	„		8 27			12 7				1 35						5C17		5 38	
Budleigh Salterton	„		9 0			12 22				1 47					3 26	5C26		6 2	
Exmouth (via Tipton St. John's)	„					12 40				2 2					3 58				
Exmouth (via Exeter Central)	„		5 50			11 43							3 16			5 11			
Okehampton	„		5 20	6 2		12 55				2 23			3 33			5 40			
Tavistock North	„			6 43		1 38				2 54			4 12			6 18			
Devonport King's Road	„			7 23		2 16				3 25			4 38			6 48			

DOWN — SATURDAYS—continued / SUNDAYS

		RB pm	pm	RC pm	pm	RC pm	RC pm	RC pm	am	RB am	am	am	RC am	RC am	RC pm	RC pm	RC pm	RC pm	pm
LONDON Waterloo	dep	3A 0	3 5		5 0	6A 0		7A 0	1 30	9A 0	1045		11A 0	11A15			4A 0	6A 0	8 12
„ Paddington	„			3A30			5A50					11A 0			1E20	3A30			
Salisbury	arr	4 41	4 51		7 0	7 45		8 25	3 40	10 50	1212		12 47	1 1			5 44	7 42	9 59
Yeovil ⎰ Junction	„	5N57	5 57		8 14	8 48		9 15	5 11	11 37				1 49			6 39	8 45	11 20
⎱ Town	„	6N 9	6 9		8 29	9 0		9 24	5 30	11 46				2 0			6 56	9 1	11 35
⎱ Pen Mill	„			6 1				9 23				2 16			5 35	6 49			
Lyme Regis	„	7N11	7 11			10Y22			12 35				2 51				7 37	9 49	
Seaton	„	7N15	7 15						12 25				2 40				7 33	9 37	
Sidmouth	„	6 44				10 10			1 2			2 50					8 12	10 22	
Budleigh Salterton	„	6 54				10 22						3 1					8 20		
Exmouth (via Tipton St. John's)	„	7 8				10 35						3 15					8 32		
Exmouth (via Exeter Central)	„								10 51			1 24						10 47	
Okehampton	„	7 27						11 17	1 42			3 43					9 7		
Tavistock North	„	8 0						11 44	2 10			4 14					9 45		
Devonport King's Road	„	8 27						12 14	2 41			4 43					10 18		

A Seats may be reserved at a fee of 2/- per seat, upon personal or postal request to the Station Master. Early application is advisable

B On Fridays arr 9 29 pm

C On 17th and 24th June arr Sidmouth 5 38 pm and Budleigh Salterton 6 2 pm

D Until 19th August dep 1A20 am. Arr Salisbury 3 10 am

E Via Swindon

F Fridays only. On Mondays, Tuesdays and Thursdays arr 10 43 pm by Southern or Western National Omnibus from **Axminster** Station. Times subject to alteration. On Wednesdays arr 11 38 pm by Bus from Axminster Square

G 22nd July to 5th August dep 12A25 am, arr Salisbury 2 4 am

H Arr 7 40 am 15th July to 12th August

J Applies until 14th July

K Until 8th July, also 9th September

MB Miniature Buffet Car for whole or part of journey

N Until 8th July

RB Buffet Car for whole or part of journey

RC Restaurant Car for whole or part of journey

X Mondays to Thursdays by Southern or Western National Omnibus from **Axminster** Station. Times subject to alteration

Y By Southern National Omnibus between Axminster and Lyme Regis. Times subject to alteration

② Second class only

June to September 1961.

113. The large finialled signal posts and the signal box were almost certainly provided for the opening of the line but the locomotives were of BR construction. No. 41291 is arriving with a branch line train on 17th August 1963, no. 80039 having come in earlier with through coaches from Waterloo. (J.N.Faulkner)

Sidmouth	1928	1936
Number of passenger tickets issued	30253	14916
Number of season tickets issued	174	315
Number of tickets collected	57432	37910
Number of telegrams	1947	1704
Parcels forwarded	5885	4580
Parcels received	29332	36208
Horses forwarded	3	14
Cans of milk forwarded	428	56
Cans of milk received	1517	20138
General goods forwarded (tons)	1197	829
General goods received (tons)	6982	6209
Coal, coke etc. received (tons)	12347	12058
Other minerals forwarded (tons)	216	466
Other minerals received (tons)	5107	332
Trucks livestock forwarded	22	10
Trucks livestock received	69	4
Lavatory pennies	2040	2437

114. No. 82019 departs from the shorter platform which could accommodate five coaches,
the other being capable of holding seven. Note
the different pattern of ground signals, the one
on the right being of SR design. (R.C.Riley)

115. The water column (right) was supplied from a tank on the road side. Ex-GWR locomotives did not work the branch regularly, as BR Standard engines had been introduced prior to the Western Region takeover in 1963. No. 4666 is seen with the LCGB Railtour on 7th March 1965, featured earlier in picture no. 76. (S.C.Nash)

116. The short siding to the end loading dock can be seen to have a catch point and a loading gauge. The deserted station was used by less than 40 passengers daily in the winter of 1964, rising to 100 on weekdays in the summer. On summer Saturdays it could be up to 900. (J.M.Tolson/F.Hornby)

117. Photographed on 13th March 1965, DMUs were introduced on 4th November 1963 giving regular services to Exeter via Exmouth or Sidmouth Junction. The remaining Saturday through trains were handled by type 2 diesel locomotives. (C.L.Caddy)

118. The three main buildings were still
standing in 1991. This 1988 view shows the
entrance that was last used by passengers on
6th March 1967. (A.Mott)

119. The engine shed found a new use - iron
gate manufacture - but the circular ventilation
aperture was filled in. All the buildings can be
seen from the public highway. (C.Hall)

120. The goods shed, and much of the yard,
was occupied by builders merchants after
closure. General goods traffic ceased on 6th
September 1965, but coal traffic continued
until 8th May 1967, two months after the last
passenger had left. At least the town retains
evidence of the railway which was largely
responsible for increasing its population from
3300 in 1871 to 10,000 in 1951. (M.Turvey)

MP Middleton Press

Easebourne Lane, Midhurst. West Sussex. GU29 9AZ
(0730) 813169

Write or telephone for our latest booklist

BRANCH LINES

BRANCH LINES TO MIDHURST
BRANCH LINES AROUND MIDHURST
BRANCH LINES TO HORSHAM
BRANCH LINE TO SELSEY
BRANCH LINES TO EAST GRINSTEAD
BRANCH LINES TO ALTON
BRANCH LINE TO TENTERDEN
BRANCH LINES TO NEWPORT
BRANCH LINES TO TUNBRIDGE WELLS
BRANCH LINE TO SWANAGE
BRANCH LINE TO LYME REGIS
BRANCH LINE TO FAIRFORD
BRANCH LINE TO ALLHALLOWS
BRANCH LINES AROUND ASCOT
BRANCH LINES AROUND WEYMOUTH
BRANCH LINE TO HAWKHURST
BRANCH LINES AROUND EFFINGHAM JN
BRANCH LINE TO MINEHEAD
BRANCH LINE TO SHREWSBURY
BRANCH LINES AROUND HUNTINGDON
BRANCH LINES TO SEATON AND SIDMOUTH

SOUTH COAST RAILWAYS

CHICHESTER TO PORTSMOUTH
BRIGHTON TO EASTBOURNE
RYDE TO VENTNOR
EASTBOURNE TO HASTINGS
PORTSMOUTH TO SOUTHAMPTON
HASTINGS TO ASHFORD
SOUTHAMPTON TO BOURNEMOUTH
ASHFORD TO DOVER
BOURNEMOUTH TO WEYMOUTH
DOVER TO RAMSGATE

SOUTHERN MAIN LINES

HAYWARDS HEATH TO SEAFORD
EPSOM TO HORSHAM
CRAWLEY TO LITTLEHAMPTON
THREE BRIDGES TO BRIGHTON
WATERLOO TO WOKING
VICTORIA TO EAST CROYDON
EAST CROYDON TO THREE BRIDGES
WOKING TO SOUTHAMPTON
WATERLOO TO WINDSOR
LONDON BRIDGE TO EAST CROYDON
BASINGSTOKE TO SALISBURY
SITTINGBOURNE TO RAMSGATE
YEOVIL TO EXETER

COUNTRY RAILWAY ROUTES

BOURNEMOUTH TO EVERCREECH JN
READING TO GUILDFORD
WOKING TO ALTON
BATH TO EVERCREECH JUNCTION
GUILDFORD TO REDHILL
EAST KENT LIGHT RAILWAY
FAREHAM TO SALISBURY
BURNHAM TO EVERCREECH JUNCTION
REDHILL TO ASHFORD
YEOVIL TO DORCHESTER
ANDOVER TO SOUTHAMPTON

LONDON SUBURBAN RAILWAYS

CHARING CROSS TO DARTFORD
HOLBORN VIADUCT TO LEWISHAM
KINGSTON & HOUNSLOW LOOPS
CRYSTAL PALACE AND CATFORD LOOP
LEWISHAM TO DARTFORD

STEAMING THROUGH

STEAMING THROUGH EAST HANTS
STEAMING THROUGH SURREY
STEAMING THROUGH WEST SUSSEX
STEAMING THROUGH THE ISLE OF WIGHT
STEAMING THROUGH WEST HANTS

OTHER RAILWAY BOOKS

GARRAWAY FATHER & SON
LONDON CHATHAM & DOVER RAILWAY
INDUSTRIAL RAILWAYS OF THE S. EAST
WEST SUSSEX RAILWAYS IN THE 1980s
SOUTH EASTERN RAILWAY

OTHER BOOKS

WALKS IN THE WESTERN HIGH WEALD
TILLINGBOURNE BUS STORY

MILITARY DEFENCE OF WEST SUSSEX
BATTLE OVER SUSSEX 1940

SURREY WATERWAYS
KENT AND EAST SUSSEX WATERWAYS
HAMPSHIRE WATERWAYS